The "Warriors" Path

DAVINE A. GREEN

Copyright © 2013 Davine A. Green

Earth-Energy Institute (Riggroup.green & Company LLC)
PO Box 7428 Akron, OH 44306

All rights reserved. Apart from any fair dealing for the purpose of research, criticism or review as permitted under the Copyright Act, no part of this book may be reproduced or transmitted in any form or by any means, electronic or mechanical, including photocopying, scanning, and recording, without the written permission of the copyright owners.

ISBN: 978-0615984414

CONTENTS

Author's Note

PART ONE: Establishing a Foundation

Evolution	Pg #9
Discipline	Pg #12
A Way of Strategy	Pg #16
Defining a Strategist/Tactician	Pg #20
Resistance	Pg #23
Persuasion, Intellectual Discipline, Complete Actions	Pg #25

PART TWO: Action Plans

Mental Warfare	Pg #31
Blood Oath	Pg #40
Afterwards: Live to Die!	Pg #46
About the Author	Pg #48

DEDICATION

DEDICATED TO ALL WHO SEEK TO LIVE LIFE IN PURSUIT OF THEIR OWN DISTINY, AND ON THEIR OWN TERMS!

Some people are prone to having sudden inspirations. Some people do not quickly have good ideas but arrive at the answer by slow consideration. Well, if we investigate the heart of the matter, even though people's natural abilities differ, when their thinking rises above concern for their own welfare, wisdom which is independent of thought appears. Whoever thinks deeply on things, even though they may carefully consider the future, will usually think around the basis of their own welfare. As the result of such evil thinking, they will only perform evil acts. It is very difficult for most silly fellows to rise above thinking of their own welfare.

Yamamoto Tsunenori

"You do not measure the fruit of your action. You have to measure your obligation of action. You have to find out what's the right thing to do. That is your duty. Whether you win or lose is not the issue; the obligation to do the right thing."

Vandana Shiva

Human beings take up virtue; then when virtue is lost, human beings insist on love; when love is lost, people demand righteousness; when righteousness is lost, people rely on property; when property is lost, law is sought; when law is lost, force is sought; when force is sought, all traces of civilization are lost.

Warrior Maxim

"You cannot solve the problems you face through the same mindset that caused those problems."

Albert Einstein

Author's Note

This book is the culmination of notes, thoughts, and metaphors; lessons and teaching from my journeys towards enlightenment, and the pursuits of the true way of the warrior.

It's not a self-help manual.

It's written by one seeker who's sharing his own findings of enlightenment.

It encourages other warriors to unify and unite in an all-out effort against suppression and oppression of the mind.

It encourages us to train our minds, strengthen our bodies and stand upright as men and women.

It provides a contract for living at a higher level.

It provides the strategies for living by the warrior code.

I am a ronin. I serve no master, no gods. I'm not controlled by possessions or greed. I seek not fame or exposure.

I take only what is necessary for survival, teach and expose the WAYS to those loyal, trustworthy and benevolent.

I seek not accolades, reward, or approval.

Strength is not measured by how many plates on the bench,

or how big your chest and arms are. Strength is not playing a sport or joining an army.

Strength is the true measurement of living without swaying, quivering, or deviating from the path of living on a higher level.

Strength is to stake one's claim to serve the **Mighty Wall of Warriors:**

1. Discipline

2. Benevolence

3. Courage

4. Honor

5. Loyalty

6. Veracity

7. Rectitude

8. Politeness

9. Self Control

Davine A. Green

Evolution

"The warrior a fighter, a man or is by definition woman of action, a specialist in meeting and resolving conflict and challenge. They seek out battle; fighting is what gives meaning to their lives."

Rick Fields- The Code of the Warrior 1991

    The definition above defines a warrior as being a "fighter;" someone of action; specialist in meeting conflict, challenges, and battle. I have always had a fascination with the promotion of personal "challenges" or "tests of spirit," endeavors that gauged levels of discipline and courage. For many years, the path of the warrior started as a "physical ambition." The goal was to see the path as training to achieve a certain physical level for the pursuit of sport or competition.

    The engaging in competition can also be likened to militaristic battles in which humans engage. Many athletes constantly refer to themselves as "warriors." I wanted something that wasn't about just being fit or working out; competing in some competition or fighting in some battle. What I wanted was something that could cement Spirit,

Mind, Body, Condition, and Attitude.

I asked myself "What constituted the true walk of the warrior? Do warriors exist in times of uncertainty and instability?

I needed to discover what went into dedicating oneself to practicing and living by a code; code that required an individual to take an oath; live and maintain a level of honor and courage throughout their life without the fear of loss or disaster.

I had questions, but more importantly, I had curiosity and incentive—much incentive. I had to "take the journey" to find the answers.

I find that there are no real rites of passage in Western culture. I contend that many people attempt to adopt other cultures to seek to explain the vast emptiness in their own lives.

Westerners ... Westerners' spend allot of time trying to "model" themselves after someone, so caught up in fantasy. Typically when Westerners' are caught up in gridlock or crises—mid-life or depression—they end up standing at the foot of "_____" (fill in the blank), asking themselves these questions:

1. "Who am I?"

2. "What's the purpose of my life?"

3. "Why am I depressed?"

4. "Will I ever find happiness?"

I'm convinced that the path which the real professional warrior must live by should be based on these tenets:

• The warrior (him or herself) must not receive merit or credit for the very creed or precepts he or she has sworn to uphold. Too much credit or accolades are rendered to individuals; rewards given for acts of valor or courage—but those actions of courage, valor, and discipline are themselves the real recipients of praise and reward.

• The warrior must acknowledge that by understanding what bravery "means" he or she can use it to obtain victory.

• The warrior must make discipline the main component despite the setbacks, the hardships, or the even the victories and triumphs.

• The warrior must be highly organized, have meticulous planning, and develop those plans fully to see results.

Discipline

- Discipline, today, is without any real training, or effort; taken for granted, as if it's a button within us we need to press to turn on.

"I need self-discipline."

- Then how do you propose to get it? What is the standard of measurement for "self-discipline?"

1. Do I need to attend school?

2. Read a book?

3. Take up a skill?

4. Seek a higher power?

On that note, let's say I did turn to faith and looked for guidance and strength to have more control in my life. What are my requirements, or options considering there are thousands of beliefs as well as deities?

Discipline is in no way a form of self-help, religious beliefs or new age.

The real reason discipline is an afterthought, or figure of speech versus real actions and long-term solutions—is that discipline is controlled by vocabulary—words implying a particular action taken should be taken or giving someone directions. It relates to the actions or reactions by those given instruction or command. With this vocabulary and directives, people in turn mimic, mirror, or emulate behaviors defined by the vocabulary.

• Knowing that discipline is not a curriculum, how can we teach discipline and still maintain control in our lives?

• How can we make people accountable when there is tremendous profit in suffering and division?

• How can we have expectations when we've created a reality out of fiction that we know outright is a lie?

• An institution of discipline has never existed in the first place, but to sell a lie is power, if only to a few.

• As the mindset today becomes filled with self-consumption, dysfunctional mentalities, disabilities in logic and reason, human defacement, and ridicule.

• The professional warrior, today, has to find that discipline and utilize it.

Having said this, what constitutes the professional warrior?

The word warrior has suddenly become a household word. It was supposed to mean "one who is brave." The sole purpose one pursued the path of the warrior was to further develop themselves in their arduous journey through life.

Delving even further into the meaning of the warrior; defining the warrior as someone who sought war or aggression eradicates the warrior's pursuits of enlightenment, balance, harmony, and the cultivation of Spirit/Sword (reactions) and Body.

Aggression is the source of our decaying consciousness. War has become the affliction of ideology or beliefs onto a society for the sake of gaining control, creating suppression, exploitation, and persecution of those who "resist" such control.

Fighting in battle does not make one "great warrior."

A Warrior possessed many skills other than those needed for survival against aggression. They needed to expand their knowledge so it could serve in building the path they sought to follow, finding bravery within them; against fear, doubt, insecurities, anger, dysfunctions and disorders—finding accountability, commitment, and single-minded determination.

As the warrior constantly trained their minds and bodies, they sought to understand the realms that governed the conditions of the universe and human beings. The warrior did not see the world as a threat, but realized that man's greed and destruction have created an imbalance, disease, disparity, and immense mental poverty.

Those who can diligently train—cultivate and hone their abilities—without labeling—are in pursuit of becoming professional warriors.

Those who dedicate their lives pursuing the enhancement of their skills, showing courage in the face of injustice, defending those being exploited, teaching, and influencing others by way of action and adhering to the "way," are in pursuit to becoming professional warriors.

A Way of Strategy

Ways of Strategy have been created to support many schools of thought; the way of health, the Confucius way, the way of Enlightenment, and so forth. Litanies of Ways were created to provide some form of exodus to the potential seeker.

Many warriors of ancient periods called themselves "masters of strategy," eventually within the world, the term strategist became applicable to anyone who understood the tactical applications and procedures of warfare and organization. The terms warfare and organization embraced many categories of social, political, economic, and militaristic tiers. In essence, many of these strategists were nothing more than fighters, soldiers, politicians, a con artist, scholars, writers, and entrepreneurs.

The Chinese word for strategy is "Heiho." Hei meant soldier and Ho meant form. So together we had a militarily derived definition of strategy utilized by the solider.

The "Way" or Michi in Japanese, or Tao in Chinese, was separate from the term strategy, the way was a path to a much stronger unification among warriors, and a higher purpose for which they served.

Warriors had to seek to understand the ways of strategy; principles that were difficult to define or instruct. They had to understand that in life there are actions and reactions:

According to the Yellow Emperor's Classic of the Internal, the universe is a collective of both these forces (actions and reactions). They represent two opposites of passive/assertive, or feminine/masculine: Yang and Yin. Deities, growth, warmth, light, and happiness are members of the family of Yang; death, darkness, poverty, sickness, evil and devils are members of the Yin family. Neither can exist apart from each other; there is constant interaction as it balances objectivity, personal characteristic development, and attitudinal perceptions.

The Ways of Strategy is the understanding of the continual flow of life and human conception. Life is not physical transformation, or mental development; life is from all of these inter/external entities working within nature and the universe; working in unison—continuing to work until the cessation of physical life (i.e. Heart, lungs, brain, internal organs......).

There is clear example of this in the following metaphoric statement made by Mencius:

The Universe chooses a person who shall bear great responsibility. First let him/her experience hard labor, starvation, poverty, heartbreak, deep distress, all kinds of adversity. Then his/her true capability shall be increased.

The universe, earth, air, nature and so forth, exist and will continue to exist—without human conception—they are infinite, eternal. Human life survives under these elements.

Hard labor, starvation, poverty, distress, and adversity are conditions that humanity creates.

Human life as we know it has now become a process of birth, youth, maturity, old age, death. The reward, per se, of human life is nothing more than physical stimulation or material accomplishments.

The warrior who penetrates through the bombardment of classifications, rituals, rules, roles and delusion does not seek drugs, sex, money, or the acceptance of another person's companionship for their needs; these are nothing more than mere items on a shelf. Success within the Way is through constant dedication, and consistent training. The warrior must understand why they breathe, how they grow, what impact is being placed on their being consistent; warriors must live life by accepting bravery, and be challenged by, and contends with the experiences provided by physical and material conception.

Live to Die! Living and dying are opposites as it relates to Yin and Yang. But strategically speaking, living, and dying are of concern to those who live.

- Living is through experiences and is represented by action and reaction.

- Dying is the cessation of these actions. Death only generates "reaction" from those who are living; memorials, funerals, remembrances and so forth.

- The Ways of Strategy as it pertains to life is to discern between life and experiences.

The warrior should not be challenged by his or her ego, guided by unsound expectations, negative habits, or behaviors. Warriors must realize that their companions, teachers, and masters should also adhere to the same Ways of Strategy that result in building a solid foundation, and sound actions and reactions.

Defining a Strategist/Tactician

The Strategist: Highly competent—able to develop a strategy, plans of action, and procedures that will bring success and satisfaction.

- They understand the needs of those to be served, and the materials needed to serve the cause better.

- They understand or devise the steps or plans that will be taken on the route to victory.

- They determine the timeline, or the length of time needed to complete the mission successfully.

- They are highly motivated individuals who can become enemies just as easily as they can serve as allies.

- They can look deeply into the visions or plans of others, seeing what others cannot see, bypassing those who assume they know "everything" or carry a "superiority" complex.

- They can lose patience dealing with stagnation or mediocrity. They can withdraw from communicating their plans, so their mission becomes more solidified with stealth and accuracy.

- They can handle the obstacles that lay in front and are unseen, and can be benign, cold, and utilize complete "objectivity" when dealing with people, and the mission.

- The warrior/strategist is a very formidable opponent; they must possess these strategic skills and constantly train in them day and night.

One must remember that the enemies of the mind, which we define as: Fear, doubt, hesitation, confusion and surprise (our main perpetrators), coupled with anger, weakness, deception, and so forth, possess these skills also, and can work to defeat even the simplest tasks. Consequently, the warrior must constantly study tactics, plans and battles that have preceded them. They must study the strategic plans with a clear and open mind, studying both pros and cons of every situation and drawing parallel structures to understanding the successes, and defeats of every battle engaged.

Warrior/Tactician

- The Tactician: Can be considered the most "uncaring."

- They can shun from receiving too much information; take an ardent attitude of "Tell me what you want me to do and when."

- They can be uncaring of the objectives or visions of others, and even the strategy. The main focus will only be on what the task is that needs to be carried out.

- Do not negate that they can serve as warriors and strategists; possess considerable degrees of knowledge and intelligence, but they train, and train constantly in all tactics and methods; highly capable of carrying out the task assigned.

- They are "short-term" in what they do. When engaged seek only one destiny, and that's victory.

- Both forward progress and backwards motions of plans, actions and implementations play major roles.

- When cross-trained, they are the worthiest of allies or foes.

The Professional Warrior must have soundness within the body-mind /mind-body, not becoming complacent or pacified; strategic as well as tactical.

Resistance

- Resistance: 1. The act of opposition to the actions taken by one individual or group to another. 2. Dissatisfaction of not being able to further progress or change conditions for all to benefit.

Under these conditions we have what is called:

- Influencing Factors- These factors sway an individual to join the resistance movement. Many of these factors can lead to confrontation.

Resistance is fuelled by:

- Motivation - Strong individual motivation is essential to the foundation of resistance, although some individual motives are not ideal and if openly expressed can do more harm than good.

What makes a person become dissatisfied and want change?

- Ideology - Many individuals have developed STRONG ideological motives for taking up cause. These ideologies take root in two broad areas, political and religious. The individual tends to subordinate his/her own personality to these ideologies; working constantly and solely for political or religious causes. In some, motivations are extremely strong.

- Fear - Many individuals become part of a movement through no personal desire of their own; joining or complying out of fear of reprisal against them.

- Chance for Success - One will join if they feel the chance for success is realistic. Individuals must feel that active participation will increase chances of obtaining power, influence and recognition.

- Guidance – The movement will stand or fall on the caliber of leadership. Understanding the environment and motives of those who resist will aid in obtaining an optimistic view for success.

What motivates and stimulates oppression?

No effort on the part of the resistor to fight oppression—Instead of an attack by the resistor on the resistor. The professional warrior must create effective methods of recruiting, and training other warriors; sharing perspectives from other schools of thought—fostering understanding; dismantling stereotypes within cultures.

Resistance does not come by force or demand—but by placing greater responsibility for the well-being and prospering of the resistor for generations now, and those to come.

Persuasion, Intellectual Discipline, Complete Actions

Warriors must have the ability to persuade; persuasion is valuable when facing an uncertain circumstance or needing to form allegiances or alliances.

Persuasion

1. Nourish, encourage and praise the talents of the subject(s). Build trust and loyalty; engage in vigorous dialogue with the subject, always find ways to gain entrance.

2. Learn and understand the possibilities of all known vices and weaknesses; engagements in negative behaviors that could exist when entering into unknown territories.

3. Makes suggestions without looking for immediate response; feelings and emotions have no influence. The desire might be strong to possess, control and gain access to resources, pushing too hard can create alienation or suspicion.

4. Learn the history, experiences, interactions, and relationships of the subject(s) you seek to align.

5. Script his or her interactions—what to say, how the subject(s) might respond and react to sensitive questions or actions.

6. Possess a cause, a need or movement which they realize

needs support. Subject(s) may give in without effort, but this does not prevent the subject from manipulating the movement after they've gained position.

7. Realize the passive or vulnerable sides of the subject(s); subjects who succumb to wants will offer resources. The subject will never question activities as long as needs filled. Caution! If the subject(s) detects being used or misled, the result could be a lashing out or physical confrontation and denouncement of the movement.

8. Establish a framework of personal perspective versus movement. The movement operates on strong beliefs and principles. What makes the subject(s) want to join the cause?

9. Pressure and consistency: The need for subject(s) to understand why their perspectives are important to the movement and its needs.

These persuasions are critical to the warrior's development and ability to accomplish their objectives, and should be studied carefully.

Intellectual Discipline

Follow these principles

- If you cannot live by a desire to speak the truth, speak not.

- Never pretend to be something you're not, laugh at something that isn't funny, or label something complicated when it's simple.

- Never learn something inadequate, use big words when you lack their meaning, or fight for causes when the people are weak and scared.

- Avoid ignorance at all costs.

- Never struggle for power or become a tool for destruction.

Intellectual Discipline is not hobby or recreation. It provides a sense of belonging; demonstrated by fellowship with other practitioners. You must think freely, feel in unison, and act cohesively. This action must create a distinction between you and the rest of humanity. You must understand the differences between internal and external motivations, letting the desires of your heart seek health, strength and stability, rather than foolish acts that harm and destroy.

Complete Actions

- Complete View
- Complete Understanding
- Complete Speech
- Complete Actions
- Complete Vocation
- Complete Application
- Complete Recollections
- Complete Contemplation

- Complete View – You should make every attempt to have a reason for your actions, behaviors, and outcomes experienced.

- Complete Speech – Learn to think before speaking; if it is not necessary to speak, don't.

- Complete Action – finish what you start; seek positive outcomes from every endeavor.

- Complete Vocation – learn and study those things that inspire you to ascend to a more productive future built on sound efforts.

- Complete Application – Apply all aspects of effort and concentration to what you do.

- Complete Recollection– Bring yourself into a whole frame of reference. The requirement here is to develop your entire self fully.

- Complete Contemplation – Learn to think; study carefully before acting out, creating harm.

Complete Actions enable one to straighten up their thoughts, how they learn; it entails a rebuilding for the pursuit of strengthening and unifying mind, technique and body.

Study these principles and train in them day and night.

PART TWO: Action Plans/Mental Warfare

Mental Warfare

One must constantly seek to train in the development of unifying Spirit, Technique, and Body.

- Spirit/Sword (mind) – Should never succumb to illness, weakness, stupidity, disorder, dysfunctions, addictions, or afflictions.

- Techniques – The usage of complete actions in all of your speech and actions. Techniques are verbal (words) directives directed towards you, and statement made about you.

- Body – That which comes up under physical attack and mental suggestions.

For complete unification of all three, one must:

- Be strong and be fully charged.

- Be accurate when directing focus and attention to the completion of efforts that will produce results.

- Continue to maintain balance, coordination, and vitality within the body.

- Be mindful of your speech.

One must learn to press down, take control, knock aside, and neutralize your opponents. Dispense with techniques that are not complete or sound; stop actions that are poisonous to mind and body. To dominate over addictions, mediocrity and disorder, one must use a continual attack on the very foundations that give rise to addiction or disorder.

The lack of continual attack (your excuses and weaknesses) provides an opportunity for your opponent, giving them the abilities to counterattack. Petty and apathetic responses and reactions to your life situations and circumstances remain on the defensive.

One learns to keep a proper distance from places of harm, and people who are poisonous so that they continue to dominate their opponent with their superior skills.

You must accept that your materialistic circumstances are of no importance to your well-being. Do not focus on want, need, or gain. Do not seek the praise of others or to blame others for the outcomes you face in the physical and material realms.

• Research and explore – Once you develop a foundation, seek to create a more personalized form going beyond what has been taught.

• Create and develop – Develop an objective mind looking at all circumstances clearly; remain free from rules and forms.

These are the weapons used daily by your opponents.

• Surprise – Techniques used to influence and create dependencies. These are a product of your enemies' sudden surprise. When an attacker finds a chance to capitalize by bombarding, gesturing, and diluting your foundation, they can go on to create fear.

- Fear – You surrender confidence by believing the enemy is superior or steeped in reputation that leads to doubt.

- Doubt – The act of worry, depression, insecurity, and being a coward; result in diminished discipline, confidence, courage and confusion.

- Confusion – Leads to indecisiveness, receptiveness to trickery, and foolishness.

The constant mind is your correct state of mind.

- Nothing accomplished if there is no calm.

- One must be quiet, comfortable, composed, and persistent.

- Complete but ready.

- Dead to worldly acceptance, alive in mind and body.

- Constantly training.

An attentive mind is also your correct state of mind.

> Though you may feel you've trained hard, made right decisions, and taken appropriate actions when engaged in the combative aspects of life, your posture of readiness must remain until the battle brings forth your

enemies' complete and unconditional surrender.

- Cultivate an opened mind – If your enemies' defenses are down while under counterattack, never make overly aggressive, doubt-filled, or hesitant attacks.

- Avoid opening your posture –If an enemy can see a weakness, then it can be exploited fully.

- Avoid opening in your movement – When one is rambunctious to initiate, collide or finish off their enemy, they leave themselves primed for counterattack; they are easily suppressed and are candidates to be contaminated with fear, doubt, confusion, hesitation and surprise.

When it is necessary to attack:

When you have learned to avoid the strength of your enemies' techniques, and can attack their weaknesses, it is necessary to attack. If, by any chance, your enemy loses focus, make good on your opportunity to attack.

Develop awareness to when your enemy is going to launch an attack. When the possibility of attack is imminent, immediately avoid their strength and techniques—countering effectively.

- When your enemies' mind and body; poorly postured, trained, and there is indecisiveness.

- Impatience, rush, and aggression.

- When weakness has overcome them, and their defenses

are down.

- Retreat forced upon your enemy; it is difficult for them to respond with counterattack.

- Prevent your enemies' from knowing where you plan to attack, see your enemies in their entirety.

- Be in absolute harmony when initiating attack, move as a unit.

It's an absolute mistake not to live thoroughly by complete actions!

You must not make moves without serious reflection. Do not seek to memorize a strategy, understand it. Regardless of title, degrees, wealth, or position, do not believe all you without a thorough examination, verification, and your complete understanding.

- You must understand the topography of your environment and your enemies'. Understanding this can help in establishing a solid foundation within the confines of your enemies' territories. Never abandon your well-earned position or give up position once you have penetrated deep into your enemies' camps. Never allow your confidence to be infiltrated and entrenched in mazes of calculation with no possible solution in sight. Never submit to a blockade created by fear, doubt, confusion, hesitation and surprise.

Never relax in the hours of victory, never get careless after you have engaged the enemy and advanced—the final result must be victory. There is no need to gloat in the face of victory; victory is not the defeat of your enemies', but it is a triumph over your insecurities, fear, and weaknesses. When you have created a fortified position, and weaknesses are clearly visible in your enemy's strategy, you must not settle for being content, you must now seek to create other weaknesses.

- Never modify your plan.

Regardless of how thick the fight might be, never lose sight of your general idea or your confidence. It is wrong to think too soon about what your enemy can do, or what they possess; seek to be clear in what you want to do.

Never despise the small details; often in them are the plans which will not only reveal, but enable you to gain significant position.

Seek of a plan that is reliable and sound, the requirement is not to move too quickly, or be placed out of range.

- Studying, researching, retrospect and development are not enough if you've never engaged the enemy and understood the real danger in these actions.

Real dangers stems from the following sources:

- Being left with insufficient support from other allies who are of the same mindset.

- Entering zones with no clear escape route.

- Enemies' plans for an attack are very weak and not well thought out.

- Enemies techniques are unsound and foolish.

- When they have a reputation that is more a fraud than legitimate.

- When what you face appears familiar, but is treated as foreign.

- Not understanding that the "darker side" of a dominating position requires no attachments of feelings or emotions.

- Enemies' positions are gone.

- Creating a false sense of security.

- Not paying sufficient attention to your enemies' plans, being able to view the danger from looking at it through your enemies' eyes.

- Neglecting defense while attacking.

- When faced with a multitude of questions concerning when to engage your adversaries and completely neutralize them.

- Utilize mental relaxation, and the ability to develop awareness beyond just being physical, and then one will only last long enough for the first blow to be thrown.

Combat strategy: The theoretical aspects of combat strategy have been applied and translated from human-to-human to conflict-to-conflict. There is a season, and that season is a continual training process in mind and body.

The warrior must respond to the initial attack.

To respond appropriately, the warrior must cultivate certain states:

- The state of Emptiness – Under this state one carries "nothing" in the heart, nothing in the gut, nothing in the mind. Form no bias or opinion.

- The state of Calm- One should possess the ability to influence others with the discipline obtained. Many should be overwhelmed by your presence. This state should motivate and inspire others to strive for the same levels of calm. In this state, one can perceive with clarity and look objectively at all surroundings.

- The state of Harmony- Able to resolve issues of emotion.

Utilize timing in decisions to act, always in favor of proper conducts and renewal. Maintain stability in the posture and the body. It's in your best interest to allow enemies' to use up their resources or energies in attacking your fortified positions without you being present. They believe you're behind a wall or the door, when in reality you are not. You've established an even greater position; well fortified; far from view.

Overt opposition to oppression only insinuates an enemy to suppress even more resources; it denies your access to opportunity. Creating the illusion of trust, making one feel you have the same goals and objectives, allows access to resources and gives you better positioning.

Eliminate the same methods or applications as your enemies' have been conditioned and trained to use. Analyze, dissect, and re-construct methods and applications. Use science, all that's applicable to save, construct, and initiate your action plans. Never find yourself in the strangleholds of enemy territory, flush them out and make them operate on your surfaces. Provide to them what looks like advantages and opportunities to bait them to the point of no return.

Study repeatedly and train on these principles day and night!

Blood Oath

The ***warrior*** strives to ***develop themselves*** without emulation or imitation of others. People who live life encompassed in fantasy; wanting to be like someone famous, idolizing material success, eventually end up disappointed by human frailties.

Conduct training inspires one to elevate ***conducts*** and not people. The code of conduct prevents people from creating names for themselves, images, and myths. Conducts are faceless. Honor has a name and meaning, the face supplied is yours.

As conduct training is administered, the individual warrior embraces ***"inflection."*** Inflection is where the individual quits pleading for guidance and revelation, and uses the guidance they now possess through proper conduct training and living. Take this maxim:

"Dishonor is like a scar on a tree, which in time, instead of effacing, only helps to enlarge."

- The scar relates to one's speech or actions (the concept of dishonor). In the time, we expect healing or removal of the scar, as the word effacing means, but there is no healing. What caused this? The continuous lack of honor!

- How many scars are we creating in the world today? How easy is it for people in this society to sell-out their honor, organizations for a bag of tokens.

- How many generations are we creating who are growing children up with attitudes that are vile, disrespectful, selfish, gutless, and cowardly?

- You have a serious responsibility to stabilize the foundation of your houses and all environments.

Are you ready to take a blood oath? Dip your finger or thumb in red paint to symbolize the drawing of blood. Or, if you are bold enough to draw blood, do that. Then, take this oath:

I_____ WILL have respect and uphold, and live by the following (RECITE):

1. I WILL be faithful to those who share the same passion for conducts.

2. I WILL show courage in the face of injustice.

3. I WILL have no problems with someone who embraces benevolence.

4. I WILL stop over-indulging in materialistic intercourse; idolizing humanity's lifestyles and fetishes!

5. I WILL WEAR THE ARMOR OF THE WARRIOR! It is my time to build myself, my business, organization, community, and family with conducts free from afflictions, disorders, and dependencies.

6. I WILL BRACE UP! I must realize that loyalty

provides a sense of connection; self-control provides a sense of responsibility.

7. For me to be loyal is to serve at the highest level, exercising self-control from participating in disease prone behaviors and actions.

8. I must take the lead; this is not affirmation or some resolution to make a change.

9. This is not self-help, new age, psychotherapy, or some religion.

10. This does not afflict my mind with double mindedness, insecurities, and indiscretions.

11. I must zero in on these conducts.

12. I must now live my life on a level far above miniscule physical pleasures and vanities.

13. I must strive to live beyond the sake of wealth and accumulation.

14. I must live in harmony and balance; connected within nature and the universe.

15. I must understand that harmony is not an illusion but a reality. If I truly seek to understand this, then I will train diligently in these conducts daily, and adhere to them my entire earthly existence.

IF I AM TRULY DEDICATED TO THE ABOVE AND I UNDERSTAND THAT THE COMMITMENT TO

THIS IS ARGIOUS, RIGOROUS AND IS A LIFE LONG PURSUIT, THEN I MUST NOW FACE AND PLEDGE BEFORE THE MIGHTY WALL OF WARRIORS.

- Benevolence
- Courage
- Honor
- Loyalty
- Veracity
- Rectitude
- Politeness
- Self Control
- Discipline

BY THIS, I, _____, ON THIS DAY_____ _____ OF THIS CALENDAR YEAR OF_____ TAKE THE BLOOD OATH.

(PLACE YOUR FINGER OR THUMB AND MAKE INPRINT)

ON THE TAKING OF THIS OATH, WE NOW ASK YOU TO MAKE COPIES OF THE OATH, KEEP ONE WHICH WILL NOW SERVES AS YOUR DOCUMENT OF COMMITMENT FOR YOU TO KEEP AND REFER TO.

WE ASK YOU TO FORWARD A COPY TO OUR INSTITUTE. WE SEEK WARRIORS TO UNITE IN STANDING STRONG AGAINST FEAR, DOUBT, HESITATION, SURPIRSE AND INSECURITY.

Afterwards: Live to Die

"Live to Die!" This attitude does not encourage individuals to live recklessly, be inconsiderate towards the feelings of others, or create harm to oneself or others.

None of these actions or reactions connects to the meaning of Live to Die!

Live to Die means to live one's life already having died a death from greed, selfishness, materialistic gain, narcissistic beauty, the fear of age or, the uncertainty of what happens upon death. It means to prevent the diluting of the mind with ignorance and stupidity.

Live to Die means feeling compassionate about a movement uniting the warrior— in a mental and physical way; uniting individuals from all walks of life dedicated to training and learning; to bring people together with honor, discipline, courage, and respect.

The writings here are lessons. They stem from my own belief that we've grown weary of not seeing more generations adhere to a code of conduct.

As you walk this path alone or with a few, you must walk regardless of what's said or thought about you. Establishing a system of practice takes time and patience, this is not sport or some form of recreation, but a WAY.

These are real expectations set for real seekers; irrespective of education or title; acronyms in front or behind their names, irrespective of how much money or possessions one owns or controls.

To train and devote oneself to a code of conduct makes us stronger in the mind and in our bodies—regardless of age.

"THE "WARRIOR'S PATH" is a CALL TO ACTION!

To confront greed, selfishness, materialistic gain, narcissistic beauty, and fearing age or the uncertainty of what happens upon death.

To encourage one to seek, experience, and use the strategies necessary to live life to the fullest and die without regret.

We're faced in this world with a battle; a battle against fear, doubt, confusion, hesitation, and surprise and all its combinations. The professional warrior must not only confront these challenges, but must build strong foundations and provide training to those who seek stability.

A warrior is not a soldier.

A warrior is not a survivor of some illness or disease.

A warrior is not an athlete.

A warrior is none of these—though we hear the term

"warrior" it is nearly always affiliated with the above.

The True Way of the Warrior is to LIVE TO DIE! Does not mean reckless pursuits or destructive actions or reactions; calls to serve the code of the warrior: HONOR, RESPECT, BENEVOLENCE, COURAGE, LOYALTY, RECTITUDE, POLITENESS, VERACITY, and SELF-CONTROL.

AUTHOR

Davine-Antional Green - Professional Warrior, national and international abstract artist, martial arts teacher and adept, entrepreneur, thinker, activist, author and liver of life on HIS OWN TERMS!

Climbed the fourth largest mountain and largest volcano in the world - **Mt. Kilimanjaro, Tanzania, Africa:** 1 October, 2004

Eastern United States Kickboxing Champion – 1990

Ohio Heavyweight Kickboxing Champion – 1989

AAU Freestyle Wrestling Champion – 1995

Ranked 5th nationally by the United States Powerlifting Federation – Deadlifting, 1997

Certified Instructor of Qi-Chi- Ki Gung Do

Certified Instructor of Keur Wong Gung Fu

1st Degree Blackbelt – Shotokan Karate

1st Degree Blackbelt –Je Duk Woo Kwan Gung Fu

1st Degree Blackbelt – Kumdo-Kendo

Founder and Director of Earth Energy Institute & Athletic Organization

Captain of the Qi-Chi-Ki Full-Contact Fighting Team

Member of the World Hwarang Kumdo-Kendo Association -2002- 2006

Former Drill Sergeant for a juvenile boot camp

Over 15 years in juvenile corrections as a facilitator, officer, and organizer.

Co-founder **of Rig-Green Companies** – multiple small business operations.

Author of the book: **The Quest of Mt. Kilimanjaro, 2005,** which documents the 2004 climb of the fourth largest mountain in the world.

Web addresses:

www.davine-green.com

Facebook: Davine-Antional Green

For information on books, seminars, workshops, lectures, or events contact us at:

Riggroup.green@gmail.com

earthenergyinst@gmail.com

EIE Institute

PO Box 7428

Akron, OH 44306

"HOW DO YOU BEAT A MAN THAT TRAINS HARDER THAN YOU DO? HE IS STRONGER THAN YOU, HE IS IN BETTER CONDITION THAN YOU, HE TAKES PUNISHMENT, HE PUTS HIMSELF THROUGH MORE PAIN THAN ANYONE CAN PUT HIMSELF IN, AND HE LOVES TO GET HIT, HOW DO YOU BEAT HIM... *YOU DON'T !*

The Shugyo Model of Training

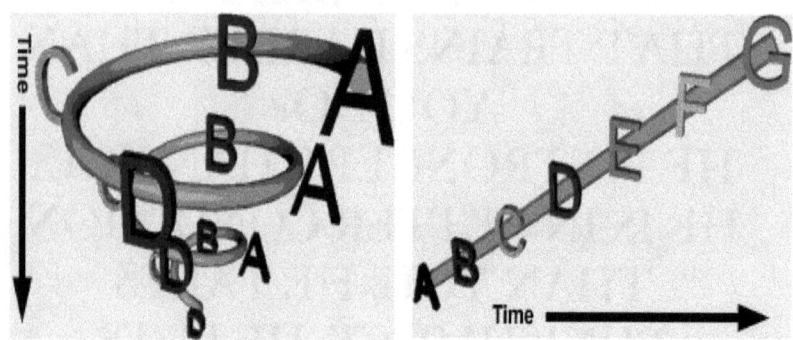

Example 1   **Example 2**

Example 1

The shugyo training paradigm is characterized by an emphasis on the **depth** of knowledge, wisdom, experience, technical ability.

In the shugyo model, the student takes only a handful of skills or forms and repeats them time and time again. Each repetition refines the skill or deepening the knowledge.

The aim here is total mastery over one's object of study and oneself to the point where both subject and object disappear into the void of experience... enlightenment.

Example 2

The western educational paradigm is characterized by an emphasis on the **accumulation** of knowledge, experiences, and skills.

In the western model—students only touch the tip of many icebergs; never achieving mastery and rarely achieving proficiency.

Hosokawa Roshi

The Paradigm for the Balance of Life

(Davine Green-2001)

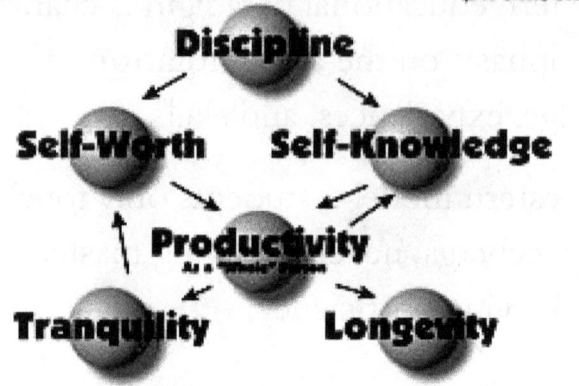

- Respect and appreciation for human values and the beliefs of others
- Developing effective work habits and learning strategies that stress self-discipline
- Developing intellectual curiosity and eagerness for life-long learning
- Appreciation for self-expression
- Spiritual/Mental/Physical health
- Utilizing time wisely
- Awareness of our own relationship within the world community

The Warriors Path

www.ingramcontent.com/pod-product-compliance
Lightning Source LLC
Chambersburg PA
CBHW050707160426
43194CB00010B/2033